The Happiness
of the People

The Happiness
of the People

Charles Murray

2009 Irving Kristol Lecture

The AEI Press

Publisher for the American Enterprise Institute

WASHINGTON, D.C.

10/24/14

Distributed to the Trade by National Book Network, 15200 NBN Way, Blue Ridge Summit, PA 17214. To order call toll free 1-800-462-6420 or 1-717-794-3800. For all other inquiries please contact the AEI Press, 1150 Seventeenth Street, N.W., Washington, D.C. 20036 or call 1-800-862-5801.

Library of Congress Cataloging-in-Publication Data

Murray, Charles A.
  The happiness of the people / Charles Murray.
     p. cm.
  "2009 Irving Kristol Lecture."
  ISBN-13: 978-0-8447-4312-7
  ISBN-10: 0-8447-4312-7
  1. United States—Social policy. 2. United States—Social conditions.
3. Happiness. I. Title.
  HN60.M87 2009
  320.60973—dc22

                                                                    2009013835

13 12 11 10 09   1 2 3 4 5

Printed in the United States of America

Foreword

Christopher DeMuth

In October 1994, just as *The Bell Curve* was hitting the bookstores, the *New York Times* published a careful smear of Charles Murray, in the form of a cover article in its *Sunday Magazine* that strongly implied that (I am being delicate here) the man was a bit unbalanced. For the cover art the *Times* dispatched a photographer to Charles's hometown in Iowa where he was visiting his parents. Several hundred pictures were taken over the course of an afternoon—many came out well, some even portrayed the subject as downright handsome. But a few shots late in the day caught him squinting into the setting sun, and in one he was unrecognizably cockeyed. Naturally, the *Times* selected that one. It ran under the headline, "America's Most Dangerous Conservative."

The incident provoked a furor in the halls of the American Enterprise Institute. Not the article or the photo—those were tired old tricks to spring on a guileless soul like Charlie. Rather, it was the headline. Jeane Kirkpatrick, Robert Bork, Irving Kristol, and probably others were thinking, "Hey, wait a minute—I thought *I* was America's most dangerous conservative!"

But the headline's premise was wrong. Charles Murray is not a conservative. He is an old-fashioned, heart-on-the-sleeve, do-gooder liberal. He is happy—I sometimes think eager—to upend the established order of things to help the poor, downtrodden, and unfortunate, and to dethrone the comfortable, smug, and well-fed. What makes him hard to categorize, and virtually *sui generis* among public intellectuals, is that he is a liberal who has avoided the two catastrophic mistakes of modern liberalism. The first is to confuse

1

the fortunes of liberty and equality with the fortunes of the state. The second is to exaggerate hugely the malleability of human nature, and thereby romanticize the possibilities of programmatic approaches to human betterment.

It was the second of those apostasies that got *The Bell Curve* into trouble. The book's capital sin was not its discussion of differences in average intelligence among racial and other groups, but rather its demonstration of the reality, durability, and pervasive social consequences of differences in intelligence among individuals. That was indeed dangerous. It meant that social engineering, like physical engineering, faced hard natural limits, and also that the modern quest for equality was, in important respects, self-defeating. But the points were so fundamental, and the evidence and arguments adduced for them so powerful, that attempting a frontal, on-the-merits rebuttal would have been problematic, to say the least. So, for many, a simpler line of attack was adopted: an effort to anathematize the author (Murray's coauthor, Richard Herrnstein, had died the month of the book's publication) and thereby render his work untouchable.

The effort failed, of course. Good books have lives of their own, and Murray's tend to be organically robust and long-lived. *Losing Ground* repays careful reading a quarter-century after its publication. *The Bell Curve*, and also *Human Accomplishment*, will be studied and debated a century after the authors and all of us have passed on. The secret of his success is that he is the opposite of the political incendiary the *Times* and others have sometimes portrayed him to be. What he is is a social scientist of relentlessly empirical bent, indifferent to the political conventions of the day and focused on bigger game, larger questions that others are missing. For Charles, econometrics is not for generating freak shows of amazing and trivial correlations, but rather for testing, explaining, fortifying our deepest intuitions and understandings from everyday life.

In many ways, the culmination of his work to date is his latest book. *Real Education* finally combines his interest in variations in innate abilities with his interests in culture, policy, and institutions. It integrates theory, fact, statistics, ethics, and direct conversation with the reader to spectacular effect. If you have not yet begun your Murray education, *Real Education* is the place to start.

Learning to live with the natural constraints of the human condition can be liberating; making practical use of those constraints can be the highest form of creativity. So it has been with Charles. Along the way, the effort has made him, and his wife, editor, and sometime coauthor Catherine Bly Cox, the most wonderful of colleagues and friends—vivacious and hardworking, principled and curious, learned and kind.

And that is real happiness, rightly understood—which happens to be his theme for the evening. Now AEI President Arthur Brooks has recently published a superlative book of his own on the subject, *Gross National Happiness*, and you may suspect that Charles is simply buttering up the new power structure at AEI. But Charles got there first, with *In Pursuit* back in 1988, and his longtime interest in the nature of happiness has been inspired by the American Founders and, most of all, by his great teacher and constant muse, Aristotle. AEI's Irving Kristol Award for 2009 is a specially bound set of the complete works of Aristotle; it is inscribed:

To Charles Murray
Exemplary social scientist
Whose measurements are means to moral understanding
Engaged Aristotelian
Who teaches of human heritage and pursuit

The Happiness of the People

My thanks to AEI's Council of Academic Advisers for this great honor.

As best I can estimate, tonight is the twentieth of AEI's annual dinners that I have attended. It has been a memorable series of evenings. There was, for example, the night in 1996 when Alan Greenspan reflected upon the "irrational exuberance" of American investors, and the next morning the Dow dropped 2 percent in the first half-hour.

The stature of the occasion has led most of the honorees to deliver a *summum* on some major theme of their life's work. On occasion, doing this has taken quite a while, and there has been not a crumb of dinner roll or a drop of wine left at any table in this room by the time the lecture ended. But more often we have been offered an intellectual treat, never more so than in 1991 when Irving Kristol himself gave his audience a dazzling tour of the horizon that integrated the cultural and political history of the West since the Enlightenment, and made it all make sense. The great disappointment of this evening for me is that Irving is not here. My greatest pleasure is that I nonetheless have an opportunity to express publicly my admiration for and gratitude to one of the towering public intellectuals of the last century, Irving Kristol.

When I began to work on this lecture a few months ago, I was feeling abashed because I knew I couldn't talk about either of the topics that were of the gravest national importance. Regarding Iraq and Afghanistan, I have not publicly said a word on foreign policy since I wrote a letter to the editor of the *New York Times* in 1973. Regarding the economic crisis, I am not an economist. In fact, I am so naïve about economics that I continue to think we have a financial meltdown because the federal government, in its infinite wisdom, has for the last two administrations aggressively pushed policies that made it possible for clever people to get rich by lending money to people who were unlikely to pay it back.

The topic I wanted to talk about was one that has been at the center of my own concerns for more than twenty years, but I was afraid it would seem remote from these urgent immediate issues. How times change. As of the morning of February 24, this is the text I had written to introduce the topic: "It isn't usually put this way, but the advent of the Obama administration brings this question before the nation: Do we want the United States to be like Europe?" And then on the evening of the 24th, President Obama unveiled his domestic agenda to Congress, and now everybody is putting it that way. As Charles Krauthammer observed a few days later, "We've been trying to figure out who Barack Obama is, where he's really from. From Hawaii? Indonesia? The Ivy League? Chicago? Now we know: he's a Swede."

In short, the question has suddenly become urgently relevant because President Obama and his leading intellectual heroes are the American equivalent of Europe's social democrats. There's nothing sinister about that. They share an intellectually respectable view that Europe's regulatory and social welfare systems are more progressive than America's and advocate reforms that would make the American system more like the European system.

Not only are social democrats intellectually respectable; the European model has worked in many ways. I am delighted when I get a chance to go to Stockholm or Amsterdam, not to mention Rome or Paris. When I get there, the people don't seem to be groaning under the yoke of an evil system. Quite the contrary. There's a lot to like—a lot to love—about day-to-day life in Europe, something that should be kept in mind when I get to some less complimentary observations.

The European model can't continue to work much longer. Europe's catastrophically low birthrates and soaring immigration from cultures with alien values will see to that. So let me rephrase the question. If we could avoid Europe's demographic problems, would we want the United States to be like Europe?

Tonight I will argue for the answer "no," but not for economic reasons. The European model has indeed created sclerotic economies, and it would be a bad idea to imitate them. But I want to focus on another problem.

My text is drawn from *Federalist 62*, probably written by James Madison: "A good government implies two things: first, fidelity to the object of government, which is the happiness of the people; secondly, a knowledge of the means by which that object can be best attained." Note the word: happiness. Not prosperity. Not security. Not equality. Happiness, which the Founders used in its Aristotelian sense of lasting and justified satisfaction with life as a whole.

I have two points to make. First, I will argue that the European model is fundamentally flawed because, despite its material successes, it is not suited to the way that human beings flourish—it does not conduce to Aristotelian happiness. Second, I will argue that twenty-first-century science will prove me right.

----- ❦ -----

First, the problem with the European model, namely: It drains too much of the life from life. And that statement applies as much to the lives of janitors—even more to the lives of janitors—as it does to the lives of CEOs.

I start from this premise: A human life can have transcendent meaning, with *transcendence* defined either by one of the world's great religions or one of the world's great secular philosophies. If *transcendence* is too big a word, let me put it another way: I suspect almost all of you agree that the phrase "a life well-lived" has meaning. That's the phrase I'll use from now on.

And since *happiness* is a word that gets thrown around too casually, the phrase I'll use from now on is "deep satisfactions." I'm talking about the kinds of things that we look back upon when we reach old age and that let us decide we can be proud of who we have been and what we have done. Or not.

To become a source of deep satisfaction, a human activity has to meet some stringent requirements. It has to have been important (we don't get deep satisfaction from trivial things). You have to have put a lot of effort into it (hence the cliché "nothing worth having comes easily"). And you have to have been responsible for the consequences.

There aren't many activities in life that can satisfy those three requirements. Having been a good parent. That qualifies. A good marriage. That qualifies. Having been a good neighbor and good friend to those whose lives intersected with yours. That qualifies. And having been really good at something—good at something that drew the most from your abilities. That qualifies. Let me put it formally: If we ask what are the institutions through which human beings achieve deep satisfactions in life, the answer is that there are just four: family, community, vocation, and faith. Two clarifications: "Community" can embrace people who are scattered geographically. "Vocation" can include avocations or causes.

It is not necessary for any individual to make use of all four institutions, nor do I array them in a hierarchy. I merely assert that these four are all there are. The stuff of life—the elemental events surrounding birth, death, raising children, fulfilling one's personal potential, dealing with adversity, intimate relationships—coping with life as it exists around us in all its richness—occurs within those four institutions.

Seen in this light, the goal of social policy is to ensure that those institutions are robust and vital. And that's what's wrong with the European model. It doesn't do that. It enfeebles every single one of them.

Put aside all the sophisticated ways of conceptualizing governmental functions and think of it in this simplistic way: Almost anything government does in social policy can be characterized as taking some of the trouble out of things. Sometimes, taking the trouble out of things is a good idea. Having an effective police force takes some of the trouble out of walking home safely at night, and I'm glad it does.

The problem is this: Every time the government takes some of the trouble out of performing the functions of family, community, vocation, and faith, it also strips those institutions of some of their vitality—it drains some of the life from them. It's inevitable. Families are not vital because the day-to-day tasks of raising children and being a good spouse are so much fun, but because the family has responsibility for doing important things that won't get done unless the family does them. Communities are not vital because it's so much fun to respond to our neighbors' needs, but because the community has the responsibility for doing important things that won't get done unless the community does them. Once that imperative has been met—family and community really do have the action—then an elaborate web of social norms, expectations, rewards, and punishments evolves over time that supports families and communities in performing their functions. When the government says it will take some of the trouble out of doing the things that families and communities evolved to do, it inevitably takes some of the action away from families and communities, and the web frays, and eventually disintegrates.

If we knew that leaving these functions in the hands of families and communities led to legions of neglected children and neglected neighbors, and taking them away from families and communities led to happy children and happy neighbors, then it would be possible to say that the cost is worth it. But that's not what happened when the U.S. welfare state expanded. We have seen growing legions of children raised in unimaginably awful circumstances, not because of material poverty but because of dysfunctional families, and the collapse of functioning neighborhoods into Hobbesian all-against-all free-fire zones.

Meanwhile, we have exacted costs that are seldom considered but are hugely important. Earlier, I said that the sources of deep satisfactions are the same for janitors as for CEOs, and I also said that people needed to do important things with their lives. When the government takes the trouble out of being a spouse and parent, it doesn't affect the sources of deep satisfaction for the CEO. Rather, it makes life difficult for the janitor. A man who is holding down a menial job and thereby supporting a wife and children is doing something authentically important with his life. He should take deep satisfaction from that, and be praised by his community for doing so. Think of all the phrases we used to have for it: "He is a man who pulls his own weight." "He's a good provider." If that same man lives under a system that says that the children of the woman he sleeps with will be taken care of whether or not he contributes, then that status goes away. I am not describing some theoretical outcome. I am describing American neighborhoods where, once, working at a menial job to provide for his family made a man proud and gave him status in his community, and where now it doesn't. I could give a half dozen other examples. Taking the trouble out of the stuff of life strips people—already has stripped people—of major ways in which human beings look back on their lives and say, "I made a difference."

I have been making a number of claims with no data. The data exist. I could document the role of the welfare state in destroying the family in low-income communities. I could cite extensive quantitative evidence of decline in civic engagement and document the displacement effect that government intervention has had on civic engagement. But such evidence focuses on those near the bottom of society where the American welfare state has been most intrusive. If we want to know where America as a whole is headed—its destination—we should look to Europe.

Drive through rural Sweden, as I did a few years ago. In every town was a beautiful Lutheran church, freshly painted, on meticulously tended grounds, all subsidized by the Swedish government. And the churches are empty. Including on Sundays. Scandinavia and Western Europe pride themselves on their "child-friendly" policies, providing generous child allowances, free day-care centers, and long maternity leaves. Those same countries have fertility rates far below replacement and plunging marriage rates. Those same countries are ones in which jobs are most carefully protected by government regulation and mandated benefits are most lavish. And they, with only a few exceptions, are countries where work is most often seen as a necessary evil, least often seen as a vocation, and where the proportions of people who say they love their jobs are the lowest.

What's happening? Call it the Europe syndrome. Last April I had occasion to speak in Zurich, where I made some of these same points. After the speech, a few of the twenty-something members of the audience approached and said plainly that the phrase "a life well-lived" did not have meaning for them. They were having a great time with their current sex partner and new BMW and the vacation home in Majorca, and saw no voids in their lives that needed filling.

It was fascinating to hear it said to my face, but not surprising. It conformed to both journalistic and scholarly accounts of a spreading European mentality. Let me emphasize "spreading." I'm not talking about all Europeans, by any means. That mentality goes something like this: Human beings are a collection of chemicals that activate and, after a period of time, deactivate. The purpose of life is to while away the intervening time as pleasantly as possible.

If that's the purpose of life, then work is not a vocation, but something that interferes with the higher good of leisure. If that's the purpose of life, why have a child, when children are so much trouble—and, after all, what good are they, really? If that's the purpose of life, why spend it worrying about neighbors? If that's the purpose of life, what could possibly be the attraction of a religion that says otherwise?

The same self-absorption in whiling away life as pleasantly as possible explains why Europe has become a continent that no longer celebrates greatness. When life is a matter of whiling away the time, the concept of greatness is irritating and threatening. What explains Europe's military impotence? I am surely simplifying, but this has to be part of it: If the purpose of life is to while away the time as pleasantly as possible, what can be worth dying for?

I stand in awe of Europe's past—which makes Europe's present all the more dispiriting, and should make it something that concentrates our minds wonderfully, for every element of the Europe syndrome is infiltrating American life as well.

We are seeing that infiltration appear most obviously among those who are most openly attached to the European model—namely, America's social democrats, heavily represented in university faculties and the most fashionable neighborhoods of our great cities. There are a whole lot of them within a couple of Metro stops from this hotel. We know from databases such as the General Social Survey that among those who self-identify as liberal or extremely liberal, secularism is close to European levels. Birthrates are close to European levels. Charitable giving is close to European levels. (That's material that Arthur Brooks has put together.) There is every reason to believe that when Americans embrace the European model, they begin to behave like Europeans.

———— ✺ ————

This is all pretty depressing for people who do not embrace the European model, because it looks like the train has left the station. The European model provides the intellectual framework for the social policies of the triumphant Democratic Party, and it faces no credible opposition from Republican politicians. (If that seems too harsh, I am sure that the Republican politicians in the audience will understand when I say that the last dozen years do raise a credibility problem when we now hear you say nice things about fiscal restraint and limited government.)

And yet there is reason for strategic optimism, and that leads to the second point I want to make tonight: Critics of the European model are about to get a lot of new firepower. Not only is the European model inimical to human flourishing; twenty-first-century science is going to explain why. We who think that the Founders were right about the relationship of government to human happiness will have an opening over the course of the next few decades to make our case.

The reason is a tidal change in our scientific understanding of what makes human beings tick. It will spill over into every crevice of political and cultural life. Harvard's Edward O. Wilson anticipated what is to come in a book entitled *Consilience*. As the twenty-first century progresses, he argued, the social sciences are increasingly going to be shaped by the findings of biology; specifically, the findings of the neuroscientists and the geneticists.

What are they finding? I'm afraid that I don't have anything to report that you will find shocking. For example, science is proving beyond a shadow of a doubt that males and females respond differently to babies. You heard it here first. The specific findings aren't so important at this point—we are just at the beginning of a very steep learning curve. Rather, it is the tendency of the findings that lets us predict with some confidence the broad outlines of what the future will bring, and they offer nothing but bad news for social democrats.

Two premises about human beings are at the heart of the social democratic agenda: What I will label "the equality premise" and "the New Man premise."

The equality premise says that, in a fair society, different groups of people—men and women, blacks and whites, straights and gays, the children of poor people and the children of rich people—will naturally have the same distributions of outcomes in life: the same mean income, the same mean educational attainment, the same proportions who become janitors and CEOs. When that doesn't happen, it is because of bad human behavior and an unfair society. For the last forty years, this premise has justified thousands of pages of government regulations and legislation that has reached into everything from the paperwork required to fire someone to the funding of high school wrestling teams. Everything that we associate with the phrase "politically correct" eventually comes back to the equality premise. Every form of affirmative action derives from it. Much of the Democratic Party's proposed domestic legislation assumes that it is true.

Within a decade, no one will try to defend the equality premise. All sorts of groups will be known to differ in qualities that affect what professions they choose, how much money they make, and how they live their lives in all sorts of ways. Gender differences will be first, because the growth in knowledge about the ways that men and women are different is growing by far the most rapidly. I'm betting that the Harvard faculty of the year 2020 will look back on the Larry Summers affair in the same way that they think about the Scopes trial—the enlightened versus the benighted—and will have achieved complete amnesia about their own formerly benighted opinions.

There is no reason to fear this new knowledge. Differences among groups will cut in many different directions, and everybody will be able to weight the differences so that their group's advantages turn out to be the most important to them. Liberals will not be obliged to give up their concerns about systemic unfairnesses. But groups of people will turn out to be different from each other, on average, and those differences will also produce group differences in outcomes in life, on average, that everyone knows are not the product of discrimination and inadequate government regulation.

And a void will have developed in the moral universe of the Left. If social policy cannot be built on the premise that group differences must be eliminated, what can it be built upon? It can be built upon the restoration of the premise that used to be part of the warp and woof of American idealism: People must be treated as individuals. The success of social policy is to be measured not by equality of outcomes for groups, but by open, abundant opportunity for individuals. It is to be measured by the freedom of individuals, acting upon their personal abilities, aspirations, and values, to seek the kind of life that best suits them.

The second bedrock premise of the social democratic agenda is what I call the New Man premise, borrowing the old communist claim that it would create a "New Man" by remaking human nature. This premise says that human beings are malleable through the right government interventions.

The second tendency of the new findings of biology will be to show that the New Man premise is nonsense. Human nature tightly constrains what is politically or culturally possible. More than that, the new findings will broadly confirm that human beings are pretty much the way that wise human observers have thought for thousands of years, and that is going to be wonderful news for those of us who are already basing our policy analyses on that assumption.

The effects on the policy debate are going to be sweeping. Let me give you a specific example. For many years, I have been among those who argue that the growth in births to unmarried women has been a social catastrophe—the single most important driving force behind the growth of the underclass. But while I and other scholars have been able to prove that other family structures *have not* worked as well as the traditional family, I cannot prove that alternatives *could not* work as well, and so the social democrats keep coming up with the next new ingenious program that will compensate for the absence of fathers.

Over the next few decades, advances in evolutionary psychology are going to be conjoined with advances in genetic understanding, and they will lead to a scientific consensus that goes something like this: There are genetic reasons, rooted in the mechanisms of human evolution, that little boys who grow up in neighborhoods without married fathers tend to reach adolescence unsocialized to norms of behavior that they will need to stay out of prison and hold jobs. These same reasons explain why child abuse is, and always will be, concentrated among family structures in which the live-in male is not the married biological father. And these same reasons explain why society's attempts to compensate for the lack of married biological fathers don't work and will never work.

Once again, there's no reason to be frightened of this new knowledge. We will still be able to acknowledge that many single women do a wonderful job of raising their children. Social democrats will simply have to stop making glib claims that the traditional family is just one of many equally valid alternatives. They will have to acknowledge that the traditional family plays a special, indispensable role in human flourishing and that social policy must be based on that truth. The same concrete effects of the new knowledge will make us rethink every domain in which the central government has imposed its judgment on how people ought to live their lives—in schools, workplaces, the courts, social services, as well as the family. And that will make the job of people like me much easier.

But the real effect is going to be much more profound than making my job easier. The twentieth century was a very strange century, riddled from beginning to end with toxic political movements and nutty ideas. For some years a metaphor has been stuck in my mind: The twentieth century was the adolescence of *Homo sapiens*. Nineteenth-century science, from Darwin to Freud, offered a series of body blows to ways of thinking about human beings and human lives that had prevailed since the dawn of civilization. Humans, just like adolescents, were deprived of some of the comforting simplicities of childhood and exposed to more complex knowledge about the world. And twentieth-century intellectuals reacted precisely the way that adolescents react when they think they have discovered Mom and Dad are hopelessly out of date. They think that the grown-ups are wrong about everything. In the case of twentieth-century intellectuals, it was as if they thought that if Darwin was right about evolution, then Aquinas is no longer worth reading; that if Freud was right about the unconscious mind, the *Nicomachean Ethics* had nothing to teach us.

The nice thing about adolescence is that it is temporary, and, when it passes, people discover that their parents were smarter than they thought. I think that may be happening with the advent of the new century, as postmodernist answers to solemn questions about human existence start to wear thin—we're growing out of adolescence. The kinds of scientific advances in understanding human nature are going to accelerate that process. All of us who deal in social policy will be thinking less like adolescents, entranced with the most titillating new idea, and thinking more like grown-ups.

<hr />

That will not get rid of the slippery slope that America is sliding down toward the European model. For that, this new raw material for reform—namely, a lot more people thinking like grown-ups— must be translated into a kind of political Great Awakening among America's elites.

I use the phrase "Great Awakening" to evoke a particular kind of event. American history has seen three religious revivals known as Great Awakenings—some say four. They were not dispassionate, polite reconsiderations of opinions. They were renewals of faith, felt in the gut.

I use the word "elites" to talk about the small minority of the population that has disproportionate influence over the culture, economy, and governance of the country. I realize that to use that word makes many Americans uncomfortable. But every society since the advent of agriculture has had elites. So does the United

States. Broadly defined, America's elites comprise several million people; narrowly defined, they amount to a few tens of thousands. We have a lot of examples of both kinds in this room tonight.

When I say that something akin to a political Great Awakening is required among America's elites, what I mean is that America's elites have to ask themselves how much they really do value what has made America exceptional, and what they are willing to do to preserve it. Let me close with a few remarks about what that will entail.

American exceptionalism is not just something that Americans claim for themselves. Historically, Americans have been different as a people, even peculiar, and everyone around the world has recognized it. I'm thinking of qualities such as American optimism even when there doesn't seem to be any good reason for it. That's quite uncommon among the peoples of the world. There is the striking lack of class envy in America—by and large, Americans celebrate others' success instead of resenting it. That's just about unique, certainly compared to European countries, and something that drives European intellectuals crazy. And then there is perhaps the most important symptom of all, the signature of American exceptionalism—the assumption by most Americans that they are in control of their own destinies. It is hard to think of a more inspiriting quality for a population to possess, and the American population still possesses it to an astonishing degree. No other country comes close.

Underlying these symptoms of American exceptionalism are the underlying exceptional dynamics of American life. Alexis de Tocqueville wrote a famous book describing the nature of that more fundamental exceptionalism back in the 1830s. He found American life characterized by two apparently conflicting themes. The first was the passion with which Americans pursued their individual interests, and made no bones about it—that's what America was all about, they kept telling Tocqueville. But at the same time, Tocqueville kept coming up against this phenomenal American passion for forming associations to deal with every conceivable problem, voluntarily taking up public affairs, and tending to the needs of their communities. How could this be? Because, Americans told Tocqueville, there's no conflict. "In the United States," Tocqueville writes, "hardly anybody talks of the beauty of virtue. . . . They do not deny that every man may follow his own interest; but they endeavor to prove that it is the interest of every man to be virtuous." And then he concludes, "I shall not here enter into the reasons they allege. . . . Suffice it to say, they have convinced their fellow countrymen."

The exceptionalism has not been a figment of anyone's imagination, and it has been wonderful. But it isn't something in the water that has made us that way. It comes from the cultural capital generated by the system that the Founders laid down, a system that says people must be free to live life as they see fit and to be responsible for the consequences of their actions; that it is not the government's job to protect people from themselves; that it is not the government's job to stage-manage how people interact with each other. Discard the system that created the cultural capital, and the qualities we love about Americans can go away. In some circles, they *are* going away.

Why do I focus on the elites in urging a Great Awakening? Because my sense is that the instincts of middle America remain distinctively American. When I visit the small Iowa town where I grew up in the 1950s, I don't get a sense that community life has changed all that much since then, and I wonder if it has changed all that much in the working class neighborhoods of Brooklyn or Queens. When I examine the polling data about the values that most Americans prize, not a lot has changed. And while I worry about uncontrolled illegal immigration, I've got to say that every immigrant I actually encounter seems as American as apple pie.

The center still holds. It's the bottom and top of American society where we have a problem. And since it's the top that has such decisive influence on American culture, economy, and governance, I focus on it. The fact is that American elites have increasingly been withdrawing from American life. It's not a partisan phenomenon. The elites of all political stripes have increasingly withdrawn to gated communities—"gated" literally or figuratively—where they never interact at an intimate level with people not of their own socioeconomic class.

Haven't the elites always done this? Not like today. A hundred years ago, the wealth necessary to withdraw was confined to a much smaller percentage of the elites than now. Workplaces where the elites made their livings were much more variegated a hundred years ago than today's highly specialized workplaces.

Perhaps the most important difference is that, not so long ago, the overwhelming majority of the elites in each generation were drawn from the children of farmers, shopkeepers, and factory workers—and could still remember those worlds after they left them. Over the last half century, it can be demonstrated empirically that the new generation of elites have increasingly spent their entire lives in the upper-middle-class bubble, never even having seen a factory floor, let alone worked on one, never having gone to a grocery store and bought the cheap ketchup instead of the expensive ketchup to meet a budget, never having had a boring job where their feet hurt at the end of the day, and never having had a close friend who hadn't gotten at least 600 on her SAT verbal. There's nobody to blame for any of this. These are the natural consequences of successful people looking for pleasant places to live and trying to do the best thing for their children.

But the fact remains: It is the elites who are increasingly separated from the America over which they have so much influence. That is not the America that Tocqueville saw. It is not an America that can remain America.

I am not suggesting that America's elites sacrifice their own self-interest for everybody else. That would be *really* un-American. I just want to accelerate a rediscovery of what that self-interest is. Age-old human wisdom has understood that a life well-lived requires engagement with those around us. That is reality, not idealism. It is appropriate to think that a political Great Awakening among the elites can arise in part from the renewed understanding that it can be pleasant to lead a glossy life, but it is ultimately more fun to lead a textured life, and to be in the midst of others who are leading textured lives. Perhaps events will help us out here—remember what Irving Kristol has been saying for years: "There's nothing wrong with this country that couldn't be cured by a long, hard depression."

What it comes down to is that America's elites must once again fall in love with what makes America different. I am not being theoretical. Not everybody in this room shares the beliefs I have been